COVID-19

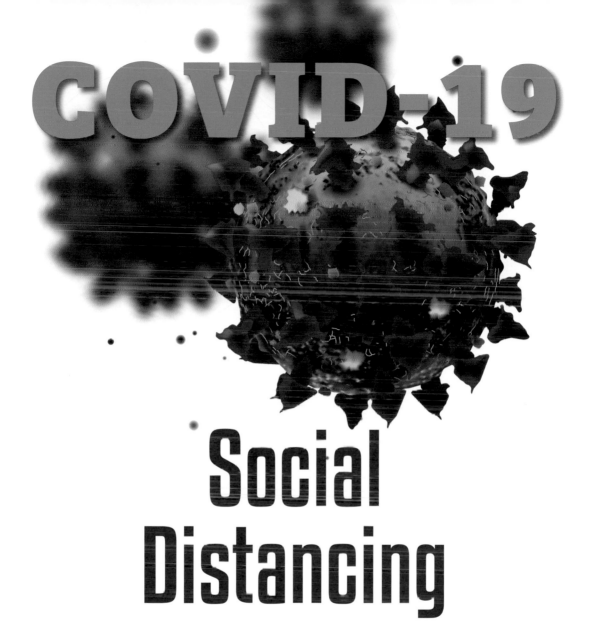

Social Distancing

by Heather DiLorenzo Williams

LERNER PUBLICATIONS ◆ MINNEAPOLIS

Lerner Publications Company
An imprint of Lerner Publishing Group, Inc.
241 First Avenue North
Minneapolis, MN 55401 USA

For reading levels and more information, look up this title at www.lernerbooks.com.

All facts and data represented in this book were accurate according to sources available as of May 2020.

Image credits: Zimniy/Shutterstock, p. 1; miljko/Getty Images, p. 3 (top); seksan Mongkhonkhamsao/Getty Images, p. 3 (bottom right); Vladimir Vladimirov/Getty Images, p. 3 (middle); zoranm/Getty Images, p. 3 (bottom left); coscaron/Getty Images, p. 5; Phynart Studio/Getty Images, p. 6; miljko/Getty Images, p. 7 (bottom); Desbarbado/Shutterstock, p. 7 (top); Sisoje/Getty Images, p. 8; Ed Freeman/Getty Images, p. 9 (left); Mike Tauber/Getty Images, p. 9 (right); Rawpixel/Getty Images, p. 11; AzmanL/Getty Images, p. 12; Michael Hall/Getty Images, p. 13; Vladimir Vladimirov/Getty Images, p. 14; frabellins/Shutterstock, p. 15; Andy Lyons/Getty Images, p. 17; Laura Olivas/Getty Images, p. 18; pinstock/Getty Images, p. 19 (top); rubberball/Getty Images, p. 19 (bottom); Chris Graythen/Getty Images, p. 20; TeraVector/Shutterstock, p. 21; miljko/Getty Images, p. 23; seksan Mongkhonkhamsao/Getty Images, p. 24; Elsa/Getty Images, p. 25 (top); Oleksii Sidorov/Shutterstock, p. 25 (bottom); eldar nurkovic/Shutterstock, p. 26; YUCALORA/Shutterstock, p. 27 (playground); SunshineVector/Shutterstock, p. 27 (cyclists); Katarinanh/Shutterstock, p. 27 (caution tape); John T Takai/Shutterstock, p. 27 (measuring tape); Visual Generation/Shutterstock, p. 27 (woman with stroller); Kondor32/Shutterstock, p. 27 (walking man); NotionPic/Shutterstock, p. 27 (woman checking phone); Denis Cristo/Shutterstock, p. 27 (crowd); Andy Lyons/Getty Images, p. 28 (bottom); Phynart Studio/Getty Images, p. 28 (middle); Rawpixel/Getty Images, p. 28 (top); Background: gaisonok/Getty Images; Cover: vectorfusionart/Shutterstock (bottom); Zimniy/Shutterstock (top); Fact icon: sinisamaric1/Pixabay

Main body text set in Minion Pro.
Typeface provided by Adobe Originals.

Editor: Lauren Dupuis-Perez **Designer**: Deron Payne

Library of Congress Cataloging-in-Publication Data

The Cataloging-in-Publication Data for *COVID-19: Social Distancing* is on file at the Library of Congress.
ISBN 978-1-72842-801-7 (lib. bdg.)

Manufactured in the United States of America
Corporate Graphics, North Mankato, MN

CONTENTS

Staying Home 4

Staying Connected 10

Learning While Social Distancing ... 16

Friends, Family, and Fun 22

Quiz 28

Activity 29

Glossary 30

Read More 31

Internet Sites 31

Index 32

Staying Home

COVID-19 was labeled a global **pandemic** in March of 2020. World leaders worked to protect people from the virus. New rules were made about how people should live. All over the world, the main rule has been "stay home!"

Some people call staying home **quarantine**. Officially, quarantine is for people who were exposed to a disease. People often go into quarantine for two weeks to see if they become sick. But people who are not sick can also self-quarantine. They stay at home most of the time. They only leave to buy food or other important items.

FLATTENING THE CURVE

Slowing the spread of COVID-19 is what helps to "flatten the **curve**." If too many people get sick at once, hospitals will not be able to take care of them all. Staying at home and social distancing help slow the virus's spread. The more slowly it spreads, the fewer people get sick at the same time. This means hospitals can care for everyone who needs help.

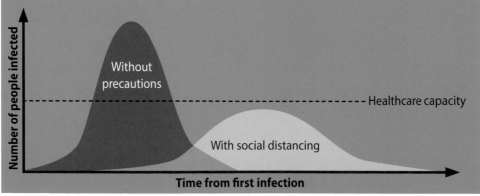

There are about 56.6 million elementary school students in the United States. Many students stopped going to school in person in March 2020.

"STAY HOME!"

STAY HOME

---

pandemic: a time when a disease spreads quickly over a large area

quarantine: keeping a person away from others to stop the spread of disease

curve: a line on a graph showing a pattern or trend in data

New Rules

COVID-19 hit the United States in early 2020. The Centers for Disease Control and Prevention (CDC) told people to stay home. The CDC also told people to stop gathering in large groups. By early April, most states had official stay-at-home orders.

A stay-at-home order means people should only leave their homes when necessary. Many businesses closed. Many people began working from home instead. **Essential workers** can still go to work. People can also go for walks outside. The CDC said that everyone should wear a mask when they go to stores. They also said that people must practice social distancing.

Many cities asked people to wear masks while shopping. This helps people protect themselves and keep other shoppers safe.

essential worker: someone whose job is important to public health, safety, and community well-being during a disaster

Social distancing is one of the most important COVID-19 rules. People who live in the same house can hug and be close to each other. They can eat and play together. But social distancing means people who do not live together must stay at least 6 feet (1.8 meters) apart.

People can still say hello as long as they are at least 6 feet apart.

Open areas are great places to go when social distancing. There is plenty of space to give people the room they need to stay safe.

DID YOU KNOW?

The US government named 16 different groups of essential workers who could continue working during the COVID-19 pandemic. They include healthcare, public safety, and food workers.

With social distancing rules in place, most businesses, like restaurants, can't operate like they normally would.

Social Distancing

Six feet is about the length of an adult's arms stretched out on both sides. This distance helps protect people from **droplets** that are spread by talking, breathing, and coughing. These droplets are how COVID-19 spreads.

Social distancing has changed the way people do most things. Grocery stores ask people to stay about two shopping carts away from each other when they are shopping. Stickers on the floor help people stay 6 feet away from each other when standing in line. Some stores limit how many shoppers can be inside at one time. Schools across the country closed. People cannot play or gather to watch team sports. Church gatherings have been canceled. All over the US and across the world, people are finding new ways to do ordinary things.

---

droplet: a very small bit of liquid

diagnose: to determine the specific illness or disease that is making someone sick

Timeline of Stay-at-Home Orders

JANUARY 20, 2020
The first case of COVID-19 is **diagnosed** in the United States.

MARCH 13, 2020
President Trump declares a national emergency in the US due to COVID-19. The CDC publishes warnings about large gatherings a few days later.

MARCH 19, 2020
California becomes the first state to issue a stay-at-home order just a few days after the CDC confirms that COVID-19 is present in all 50 states.

MARCH 24, 2020
Fourteen more states, including New York, Washington, Ohio, and Illinois, have instructed residents to stay home.

APRIL 1, 2020
A total of 34 states plus Washington, DC, have issued stay-at-home orders.

APRIL 7, 2020
South Carolina becomes the last state to issue a stay-at-home order, bringing the total to 42 states.

APRIL 20, 2020
There are still eight states without statewide stay-at-home orders.

APRIL 24, 2020
Georgia becomes the first state to lift its stay-at-home order despite warnings from the CDC.

Staying Connected

The internet has been a useful tool for many years. During the COVID-19 stay-at-home orders, it became a lifeline. Smartphones and laptops became windows to the outside world. Different **apps** allowed people to have **virtual** meet-ups.

Some apps were already built into certain phones. One app is FaceTime. Before COVID-19, people used FaceTime to talk to family members who lived far away. Now, even people who live near each other use it to catch up every day. Zoom is another app. It can be used on laptops, phones, and tablets. Many people can video chat together using Zoom.

People have also used social media apps to stay connected. Friends have used Instagram, SnapChat, and Facebook to stay in touch. They continue to share their experiences with others. This has made people feel less alone.

DID YOU KNOW?

A little more than half of American children have a smartphone by the time they turn 11. Around 84 percent of US teens have their own phones.

---

app: a small computer program, usually downloadable to a mobile device

virtual: occurring online with the help of a computer or mobile device

Once social distancing began, Zoom's daily users went from 10 million people to more than 200 million people.

Some gyms have been using Instagram and Zoom to offer live workout classes.

Keep Moving

People have found many ways to connect with others using apps and social media. Sports teams canceled in-person practice. But coaches can use Zoom to meet with teams. They can use messaging apps to meet with players. Coaches have given their players challenges to complete. They have shared YouTube videos of **drills** and practices. Some teams even required players to post videos of themselves doing daily drills.

Dancers have also used these tools. Many **studios** have used Zoom to keep teaching classes. Up to 100 people can join a Zoom meeting. This has allowed dance teachers to meet with many students at one time.

Other kinds of exercise studios have also held online classes. Yoga teachers are offering free classes. Fitness instructors are posting **sessions** online or doing live Zoom classes. Many people miss in-person practices or workouts. But these tools help them keep moving and stay connected with others.

drill: a repetitive exercise that helps someone learn a specific skill

studio: a place where artists work, or where people perform or exercise

session: a brief period of time devoted to a particular activity

EVERYONE CAN DANCE

Ryan Heffington creates dances for famous singers and TV shows. He had to temporarily close his dance studio because of COVID-19. But he started hosting free sessions on Instagram. Special guests like Pink have joined the class, which is called Sweatfest. Thousands of people watch Heffington's class and dance along with him. People have said Sweatfest has helped them feel happy during the stay-at-home orders. Heffington has found joy, too. He once said he would love to make the whole world dance. Now he is getting that chance.

Keeping up with music lessons is possible by using the internet to stay connected.

Staying Creative

Many people have used apps to keep up with a favorite **hobby**. Some have even taken up new hobbies. Musicians around the world have performed daily or weekly mini concerts. Many concerts have been shown live on Facebook and Instagram. Music teachers have taught piano, guitar, and singing lessons using FaceTime.

Well-known artists and **illustrators** have posted lessons online. Many have posted drawings that people can print and color at home. Art museums have shared ideas for making art projects using everyday items.

Art, music, and fitness are some ways people can stay connected while staying at home during COVID-19. These activities also help people stay happy and healthy. Online tools and apps give families a way to have fun during a stressful time.

---

hobby: an activity people enjoy doing in their free time

illustrator: someone who draws pictures for books, movies, or cartoons

#stayhome and...

LOOK AFTER YOUR PHYSICAL HEALTH

Eat healthy foods.

Stick to a schedule.

Avoid sugary drinks.

Be active for 30 minutes a day.

Bathe regularly

LOOK AFTER YOUR MENTAL HEALTH

Share your feelings.

Help each other, especially those who need it most

Create daily and long-term goals.

Find fun hobbies.

Look for opportunities in the difficulties.

Check on neighbors, family, and friends.

Learning While Social Distancing

By the end of March 2020, most US schools were closed because of COVID-19. Many stayed closed for the rest of the school year. Teachers had to find new ways to teach. They took their classrooms online.

Teachers and students have used many tools to communicate. These include some of the same tools friends and businesses use. They also include some tools made just for learning. Websites and apps such as Canvas and Google Classroom have helped schools go virtual. Students can post their assignments. They can have class discussions. Teachers can grade assignments online. They can even share videos of lessons.

Before COVID-19, most students were not allowed to use their phones in class. Now many students are using their phones to view classes. They are using them to complete assignments.

DID YOU KNOW?

During the COVID-19 crisis, many mobile phone companies gave families free data so they could use their phones for school and work.

Even though school buildings are closed, teachers are still reading to students and teaching lessons through video.

What Does Online School Look Like?

Students from kindergarten to college are taking virtual classes because of COVID-19. Some classes are live on Zoom. This allows teachers and students to see and talk to each other. Kindergarteners have show-and-tell on Zoom. Middle school math students work on problems together. College students have **debates** and discussions.

Some assignments and tests are **digital**. Students can complete them online. Others must be printed out, completed, and photographed. Students or parents send the photos to their teachers. Teachers can grade assignments and provide **feedback** online.

---

debate: a discussion between two sides with different opinions on a subject

digital: done on a computer

feedback: helpful information that tells someone how they can improve their work

In some areas, schools are providing devices to students so they can complete lessons.

Many teachers have one-on-one meetings with their students. They use Zoom or FaceTime. Young students can read to their teachers. They can do math problems together. Older students can get extra help with a subject. They can talk about books they have read.

COVID-19 has changed the way students go to school. But teachers and parents work hard to make sure their students are still learning.

Video lessons are often paired with worksheets that students complete at home.

VIRTUAL FIELD TRIPS

Zoos and museums around the world have closed because of COVID-19. Many have offered virtual visits and field trips. People can tour museums online. They can view paintings and other items up close. Some zoos have daily zookeeper talks. The keepers introduce an animal. They might feed or groom it. Viewers can ask questions online for the keepers to answer.

Challenges

At-home school has not been easy for some. Not all students have a laptop or tablet. Many have had to complete assignments using just their smartphones. Schools across the country have tried to help students get the items they need for learning. Some teachers and principals have even dropped off books and laptops to students' homes.

Even if they have a laptop or tablet, not all students have internet access. It might not be available in rural areas. Or some families may not be able to afford it. Internet companies offered free internet access in many areas. Some schools set up free **Wi-Fi hotspots** for students. Teachers gave students extra time to do their work. Many schools stopped giving students grades. Students either passed or failed for the rest of the school year.

Many schools stopped instructing students for a few weeks to prepare for distance learning. Schools tried to make sure families had the supplies they needed to be successful.

Wi-Fi hotspot: a public area where wireless internet is available

Internet Access Across the United States

Not everyone has access to the internet. During stay-at-home orders, the internet has become very important. Below is a map of the United States showing the percentage of people who do not have internet access in each state.

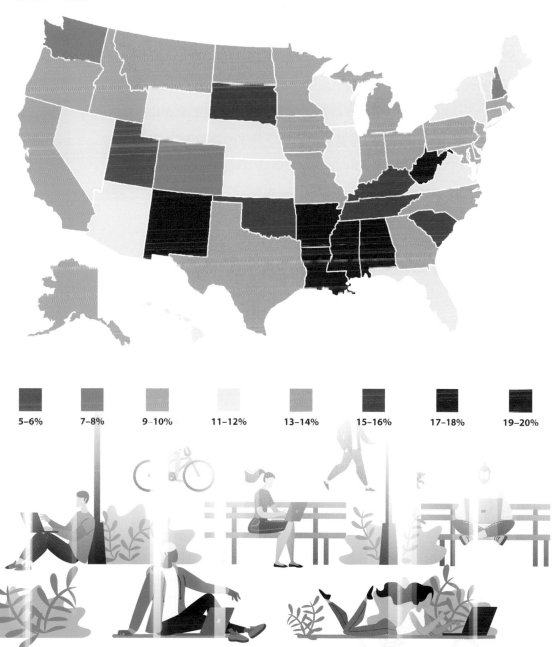

5–6%	7–8%	9–10%	11–12%	13–14%	15–16%	17–18%	19–20%

Friends, Family, and Fun

Grayson turned 12 during the COVID-19 stay-at-home orders. His parents had to cancel his laser tag party. He could not even have cake with his grandparents, aunts, uncles, and cousins. Grayson's dad decided to throw him a virtual party. He invited Grayson's friends and family to a Zoom meeting. Everyone sang to him as he blew out his candles.

Some people have used Zoom to host weddings. Many couples had to postpone their weddings because social distancing would not have been possible. Some decided to get married anyway. Their guests attended using laptops and phones. Some couples had their ministers on Zoom, too. Others said their vows outside, at least 6 feet away from the minister. These families, couples, and friends found special ways to celebrate while staying safe.

DID YOU KNOW?

Many neighborhoods across the US have had scavenger hunts during the stay-at-home orders. Neighbors place stuffed bears or other items in their windows. Kids in the area have hunted the items on daily walks through the neighborhoods.

Including family and friends in major life moments is still an important part of life when stay-at-home orders are in place.

Being Together

Many family traditions have changed because of social distancing. Easter egg hunts were cancelled. Date nights and playdates have been put on hold. Many family vacations were postponed. People have found ways to be together anyway.

Families and friends use Zoom to have dinner together. Friends can have "watch parties" on Netflix. They can watch movies at the same time and chat about them. People of all ages have used FaceTime and other apps to spend time together. Kids have had virtual playdates. Best friends have had virtual sleepovers.

Movie theaters closed while stay-at-home orders were in place. But with Netflix and other streaming services, families could still have stay-at-home movie nights.

Some families have used technology to take virtual vacations. The US National Park Service has live cameras and virtual tours of many parks. Google Earth lets people get a close-up view of places around the world. Virtual parties, trips, and dinners are not the same as real-life experiences. But during social distancing, they have given people a way to have fun together.

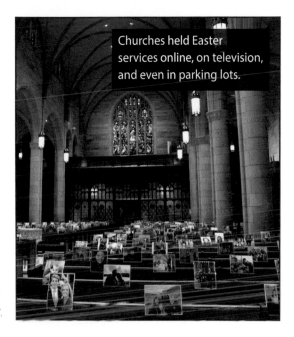

Churches held Easter services online, on television, and even in parking lots.

VIRTUAL THRILLS

Disney World and other theme parks closed because of COVID-19. But thrill-seekers can still try out roller coasters at parks across the US using a tablet or computer. People can take a virtual ride on Disney's Space Mountain or the Matterhorn. Universal Studios fans can check out Hagrid's Motorbike Adventure or the Hollywood Rip Ride Rockit. These and other virtual rides put people in the front seat of some of America's most popular thrill rides.

Getting Out

Some people have spent time together without technology. Neighbors have had picnics. They stay in separate yards and eat separate meals. Some neighbors have had dance parties. They turn up their music and dance together on their own porches. This is a safe way to be together while social distancing.

Many public beaches and hiking trails have been closed. Parks and playgrounds have been off-limits. Crowded places make social distancing hard. But some parks have stayed open. Some beaches reopened after a few weeks. Many people have visited these places. Being outside is good for people's health as long as they practice social distancing.

Finding ways to connect with others is important. By staying 6 feet apart or using a smartphone app, friends and family can be "together" and flatten the curve at the same time.

When using the same walkway as a stranger, one tip is to move to the side or wait just off the trail to allow them to pass at a safe distance.

Tips for Physical Distancing in Parks

Know what 6 feet looks like. Lay measuring tape on the ground. It's the distance of a surfboard, long yoga mat, or adult bike.

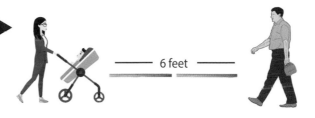

Do not use playgrounds or other frequently touched surfaces.

Use a face mask, and only go places with the people you live with.

Avoid crowded areas. If a space cannot be enjoyed safely, go home or discover a new park in your community.

QUIZ

1. What are essential workers?

2. When social distancing, how far apart should people stay?

3. On what date did President Trump declare a national emergency in the United States?

4. Name at least two apps people have used to stay connected during the stay-at-home orders.

5. What percent of US teens have their own cell phones?

6. What is one way people have stayed active during the stay-at-home orders?

7. Name at least one reason at-home school has been challenging for some students.

1. People whose jobs are important to the safety and well-being of other people
2. At least 6 feet
3. March 13, 2020
4. Zoom, FaceTime, Facebook, Snapchat, and Instagram
5. 84 percent
6. Online fitness classes, taking walks
7. No internet access, no computer or other device

SOCIAL DISTANCING ACTIVITY DIRECTORY

During a pandemic, social distancing is very important. Planning some activities that can be done during that time can help. The ideas for things to do online can be overwhelming. Create an Activity Directory just for your family. Think about things your family enjoys doing in normal times. Then make a booklet of things you can do together, either while social distancing or without leaving your house.

MATERIALS

- Computer or smartphone for internet research
- Construction or art paper
- Markers or colored pencils

STEPS

1. Make a list of at least five categories. Some ideas include Movie Nights, Virtual Vacations, Virtual Field Trips, Social Distancing Hikes, Virtual Concerts, and Family Game Nights.

2. Brainstorm some ideas for each category. Then research activities to include in your booklet.

3. Make a section in your booklet for each of your five categories.

4. Include at least five or six activities in each section. Include details for each one. For example, if you have a Movie Night section, include the location (the living room), menu (popcorn, nachos), and feature presentation (*Toy Story 4*). If you have a Virtual Vacations section, include the name of the location, a description, and anything your family members can bring to make the "trip" more exciting.

5. Illustrate your directory and make it colorful!

6. Display your directory! Leave it in a place where everyone in your family can check it out, such as on a family room coffee table.

GLOSSARY

app: a small computer program, usually downloadable to a mobile device

curve: a line on a graph showing a pattern or trend in data

debate: a discussion between two sides with different opinions on a subject

diagnose: to determine the specific illness or disease that is making someone sick

digital: done on a computer

drill: a repetitive exercise that helps someone learn a specific skill

droplet: a very small bit of liquid

essential worker: someone whose job is important to public health, safety, and community well-being during a disaster

feedback: helpful information that tells someone how they can improve their work

hobby: an activity people enjoy doing in their free time

illustrator: someone who draws pictures for books, movies, or cartoons

pandemic: a time when a disease spreads quickly over a large area

quarantine: keeping a person away from others to stop the spread of disease

session: a brief period of time devoted to a particular activity

studio: a place where artists work, or where people perform or exercise

virtual: occurring online with the help of a computer or mobile device

Wi-Fi hotspot: a public area where wireless internet is available

READ MORE

Denton, Michelle. *Pandemics: Deadly Disease Outbreaks.* New York: Lucent Press, 2020.

Gitlin, Marty. *Virtual Learning.* Ann Arbor, MI: Cherry Lake, 2020.

Glenn, Joshua, et al. *Unbored Adventure: 70 Seriously Fun Activities For Kids and Their Families.* New York: Bloomsbury, 2015.

Huebner, Dawn. *Something Bad Happened: A Kid's Guide to Coping With Events in the News.* Philadelphia, PA: Jessica Kingsley, 2020.

Parks, Peggy J. *Social Media.* San Diego, CA: ReferencePoint Press, 2017.

INTERNET SITES

https://www.livescience.com/coronavirus-kids-activities.html
This website includes a collection of virtual and hands-on activities kids and families can enjoy at home.

https://kidshealth.org/en/kids/coronavirus-kids.html?WT.ac=k-ra#catplaces
This article provides a guide to preventing the spread of germs, as well as tips for surviving the stay-home order.

https://kidshealth.org/en/teens/coronavirus-calm.html?ref=search#catplaces
This article helps kids and teens understand why social distancing is so important and how they can make a difference by following the rules.

https://www.cdc.gov/coronavirus/2019-ncov/prevent-getting-sick/social-distancing.html
The CDC's official website explains social distancing rules, the importance of disease prevention, and steps to take for those who might have been exposed to the virus.

INDEX

art 14

Canvas 16
Centers for Disease Control (CDC) 6, 9
COVID-19 4, 6, 7, 8, 9, 10, 13, 14, 16,
    18, 19, 22, 25

Disney World 25

FaceTime 10, 14, 19, 24

Google Classroom 16

Heffington, Ryan 13

internet 10, 14, 20, 21

music 14, 26

teachers 13, 14, 17, 18, 19, 20

Zoom 10, 11, 12, 13, 18, 19, 22, 24